a mother is a paperclip

with best wishes

Karen

a mother is a paperclip

by

Karen Francis

First published 2024 by The Hedgehog Poetry Press,

5 Coppack House, Churchill Avenue, Clevedon. BS21 6QW

www.hedgehogpress.co.uk

Copyright © Karen Francis 2024

The right of Karen Francis to be identified as the author of this work has been asserted in accordance with the Copyright, Designs and Patents Act 1988. All rights reserved. No part of this publication may be reproduced, stored in or introduced into a retrieval system, or transmitted in any form, or by any means (electronic, mechanical, photocopying, recording or otherwise) without prior written permissions of the publisher. Any person who does any unauthorised act in relation to this publication may be liable for criminal prosecution and civil claims for damages.

ISBN: 978-1-916830-11-0

Dedicated to Benjamin and Joanna, who continue to shape me in my organic, inexorable, evolution as a mother, especially as, with their wonderful partners, they model such great parenting themselves – and most of all to Nick, because I couldn't be the mother I am, without him being the incredible husband and father he is.

With thanks to Mark Davidson, of Hedgehog Poetry Press, for giving validation to my work

Contents

Nest is everything 9
Being Impregnable 10
15th October: Lighting candles 11
The Power of the Fragile 12
Motherhood trumps the PTA 13
The reality of early motherhood in 12 strikes 14
It's all in the small print 16
Cutting the apron strings 17
The Magnets 18
On Standby 19
All praise to Taweret 20
Maternal connections 22
Default Setting 23
Police Uniforms 24
The bitter truth of mothering an adult child in pain 26
She stands strong 27
Salt 28
A window for breakfast 29
Get beneath her skin 30
Ultimately a mother is a paperclip - 31

NEST IS EVERYTHING

world within a world
nest is　　　*everything*
for us shrill fluff-sibs
all vying for the worm

holds us safe
in wispy twig-weave,
wind-teased, it rocks us,
cradles us, cupped in familiar

until ravening hunger,
squash and squeeze,
renders it just
the curved horizon of appetite

wings itch to unfurl w-i-d-e
flight becomes a　　　**must**
nest is wind-blown threadbare, left
without second glance　　done its job

wing-s-t-r-e-t-c-h until
a deep home-hunger is recognised
as the *missing egg*　　construct nest
spit feathers to line it with all you have

form own *world within a world*
because nest is　　*full-on* ***everything***
for us and our fluff-babes, even beyond
when their wings itch to unfurl wide

learn to glide the thermals
when empty nested
new winds for old wings
yet still, nest is　　simply, ***everything.***

BEING IMPREGNABLE

1. The waiting room holds itself tight, like that still, airless, moment
before storm breaks, despite attempts at comfort, deep, soft, armchairs
and coffee maker in the corner, this is not a place of ease. Skin crawls
in the predatory silence. Neck whips round with every door opening, in case this *is it-*
   this is my person in white coat and plastic smile
   this is the point of being told, viable or
   not.
   Again
Above my head clouds are massing, roiling, darkening the room to tomb-state,
filling with precipitation, pre-deluge. Even though I've been here so many times,
hands are clammy, don't know what to do with themselves,
   and the door opens
   and the rain hurls down flattens, guts and obliterates me.
   Again.

2. I am an *impregnable fortress*, he says, squinting up from the thick wad of notes
that carries our hopes and dreams in leaking boats, swept along in a typhoon of ink,
documenting myriad test results. He proffers tissues, tries awkwardly to explain
   You see, the fertilised embryos can sneak past the outer guards
   but trying to take the castle, get repelled, and expelled
   again.
 So, let's build a trebuchet, I counter, *change tactics, generals, try subterfuge?*
   He blanches, claims he doesn't have a military background. But Nature and I do.
   I don a lifebelt, step up on mission once more, rally troops,
   and continue to give it all I have. I weaponise.
   Again.

15TH OCTOBER: LIGHTING CANDLES

I cast my grief out
to be snatched by wind,
    hidden within its chill wailing,
    to be nursed, to be swaddled in dark,
and light seven small, but significant, candles.

          She nests in the corner of the sofa,
          crochet coils in idle hands,
          empty eyes occasionally lift to the lambent light,
          here- but not present.

Tonight, writhing memory-worms
summon speculative *what-ifs-*
    to rise phoenix-like,
    in defiance of their pre-emptive leaving -
        Blonde? His curls? Tall like him, or short like me?
        They play amongst the licks of candle flame
        before vanishing once more with the smoke.

          As the candlelight judders and coughs
          she fumbles with the hook, twists yarn,
          forms more rows of knots, on mission,
          making delicate, fragile, things.

(Note: 15th October is Pregnancy and Infant Loss Remembrance Day, a day to remember babies who died during pregnancy or as new-borns)

THE POWER OF THE FRAGILE

A day they said we would never see is **this day. Is now.**
Cradling my new-born – so precious, and so desperately wanted,
I dismiss the ache-tear of body as irrelevant,
will wear my abdomen's permanent smile with pride, joy.
My husband's eyes glisten as he, so carefully, tenderly, enfolds us
one hand around the babe, one hand gently caresses me –
creating a bonded skin-to-skin everlasting circle.

Placing him gently between us, we gaze down -
>
> breath-taking-beautiful
> perfectly formed small person
> smooth feather-soft-skin
> peachy-curve cheeks, all rounded contours,
> exquisite, tiny hands beginning to reach out
> splayed fingers - long, musician's fingers.
> Pearl toes fringe petite, plump feet
> scrunching downy blanket, exploring.
> He is eerily, unexpectedly, silent –
> when   *lightning bolt*
> shock-startling sky-eyes, pin me in place,
> weighing my worth, seizing connection, ownership -
> **willing me**   to *pick up, hold secure*.

Inside, a new dedicated heart-room unlocks
for this miracle child,
his name engraved on the door,
and I am his now,
always and forever.

MOTHERHOOD TRUMPS THE PTA

Rigor-mortis-like fixed-smile in place, each breath forms clouds.
Despite three pairs of socks, feet burn with cold
from the icy lake-puddle I stand in to serve these sodding hot-dogs.
I stuff misery down inside the envelope of me,
mechanically trill *Thank-you, enjoy!* through chattering teeth.

With each ear-splitting battery of rockets, screams ricochet across the school field
from my two-year-old - who hates the noise, the crowds and could care less
about fireworks - yet I seem to end up here every November 5th -
and she claws up my legs frantic for a *pickup*, to be *held safe* as I try
to force a non-compliant sausage in a bun – showering us both with onion gloop.

I gather her up in her full melt-down mode,
multi-layers making for a tricky hug position.
Her little face shiny with freeze-dried tear tracks,
she oozes upset, sobs noisily and snottily into my neck.
And my mother-heart snaps.

I holler to the beneficently smiling, self-proclaimed queen of the PTA,
swigging mulled wine as she holds court at the bonfire,.
Hey Ruth! Sorry – grab this pinny -you're going to have step in, I'm taking Jo home!
        But I... can't you just...
No.   *Going now.*
And I toss the greasy apron at her, and stalk, head high, an Amazon
carving through the *ooh* and *aah-ing* crowd, like Moses parting the Red Sea,
and sail through the school gate, damp child-bundle in arms.

I'm sorry. Never again Jo-baby, I promise.
Bubble bath and hot chocolate in our jammies, eh?
Just you and me, babe.

THE REALITY OF EARLY MOTHERHOOD IN 12 STRIKES

After midnight, when the clock strikes 1
those just gone to bed, hold wine glass heads, ringing inside-outside
because they can still remember the impossibility of how much there is to do tomorrow

when the clock strikes 2
plumbing turns pathfinder, water flushes and gurgles through every pipe in the house,
a child screams *Mummy!* -and night-widdlers, trying so hard to be silent, failed. Again.

when the clock strikes 3
it is answered by the owl in the oak tree, that taps the kitchen window, that harmonises
with every buffet of wind, the garden gate banging drum and the fox's harsh-eerie bark.

when the clock strikes 4
it ignites snoring that rises rumbling from hell-pits, like a surge of howling Orcs, clashing
sword to shield, which probably accounted for much body-heaving and elbow jabbing.

when the clock strikes 5
small elephant feet patter, piping voices encourage each other to *shh-quiet,* tiny fingers
pry up eyelids to see if victim is *'wake-yet?'* Gasps explode on opening eyeball-to-eyeball.

when the clock strikes 6
kettle is refilled, CBeebies incites creative stickiness in the lounge involving a rice-crispy-
and-buttered-toast bedecked sofa, head thumps with washing-machine drum hiccup

when the clock strikes 7
whirlwinds tear through the house banging at bathroom doors to demand priority use
seize eatables from any unguarded plate mid-hurtle to the door -some even shout *Bye!*

when the clock strikes 8
cardboard creations stick fast to kitchen table, floor flashes iridescent glitter, and small
scientists research if bath-bombs remove glue from stuck-together-fingers. They don't.

when the clock strikes 9
smalls demand second breakfast with menaces. Despite ransacking - *no paracetamol*
(not even in with the cookie cutters). Starving ones are thrown the last of the sliced loaf.

when the clock strikes 10
shopping delivery arrives, and towers in a magnificent mountain - between front door and
rest of house, where muddy-wellied-kids run over fresh-washed kitchen floor and lounge.

when the clock strikes 11
mites nap after ferrying shopping to kitchen, in a convoy of wheeled toys - and the eggs
were probably superfluous anyway. Coffee was missed off the order. Crying happened.

when the clock began to strike 12
everyone is singing wheels on the bus, with full action movements, tricky when driving-
but keeps you awake, because *when the clock finishes striking* it reverts to default -
exist on fumes through afternoon and evening, trying to ensure no one dies -
until folk under a metre in height finally collapse into bed, (usually not their own),
and adults succumb to sofa, and some days, *alcohol*, even on a Wednesday-
until it all starts again.

IT'S ALL IN THE SMALL PRINT

My hands clench tight
to the essential threads of life,
prevent them unravelling, tease them
back into warp and weft, take care
of the little details, weave recognisable cohesion
from the security of the familiar.

I deal with the little bumps in the road-
prepare the favourite meal, the cake
lying in readiness to bolster
the cure-all-cup-of-tea,
always have a bed ready, crisp, clean
sheets, scented with freesias, dried in honest fresh air,
the midnight conversations, soft-voiced
supportive phone calls, unquestioning
assistance with form filling, transport, whatever -
I sit on my opinions, try to just listen.

My **all** holds tight
to the small stuff of life,
continues to weave together
that warm, nurturing blanket
here to comfort you, whether you are three, or thirty-
ease your passage, offer a brief window
to pause, reset, breathe.
It's the job.
It's all in the small print.

CUTTING THE APRON STRINGS

Plaintive mooing
lured me to the bottom of the garden.
Both Friesian mothers, stiff as bed frames,
stood, necks stiffly distended
venting distress to the iron sky,
steam rising from their broad, kitchen-table backs
as they bellowed their worry-call.

The two calves
grown cheeky and adventurous
had inveigled through paddock security,
to munch illicit grass in my neighbour's garden,
out of parental line-of-sight, stood
undaunted by their mothers' vocal concern –
in typical, adolescent *talk to the tail*.

Phone call to farmer, quick fence-fix,
mothers and offspring were reunited.
Next day, the cows summoned me
with that same siren call, noising their fear
as they fence-pushed anxiously,
usual placidity unravelling by the minute -
as the oblivious calves ... were back in the garden.

The taste of a child's freedom isn't easily swallowed
back down - the best you can hope for
is that you've prepared the path to independence well-
and that they occasionally remember
to look back and wave.

THE MAGNETS

Hot and sultry
the day before they got married,
taking a snatched free moment sprawled on the lawn,
caught in the strange between-time of now and *after* -
my beautiful, ethereal, curly-haired daughter,
        a slight dryad in short, blue-striped sundress,
        with her strong sapling oak, groom to be,
whose eyes couldn't help but find hers
like a helpless homing pigeon.

He drank her in as if desert parched, wore his heart
emblazoned across taut young frame,
worshipped her with every fibre.

Oblivious to the world around them
mutual adoration spilt from the two of them,
always one with hand lightly resting on the other,
stroking, feathering along the arm, legs -
        smiles fixed, as though their faces would break
        before they would let them drop.
Sensual static built in the ether charged around them,
built, to be almost tangible, heralding a thunderstorm,
that would break if release was held back for much longer.

And only because it was **right**, because he had made abundantly clear
he believed his role, his core function from now on
was to care for her to the best of his ability- could I let her fly -
support this new fledgeling independent state.
See me now - a mother, raw hearted, teary, but   **letting go.**

ON STANDBY

The vacuum cleaner sulks in the corner, desperate for *walkies*, and all through the house electrical appliances conspire to drive me crazy with their incessant bullying beeps to call me to heel. But I'm **on standby**. I'm tied to the phone, can't risk not hearing it, because I'm **on standby**. It's her due date today and my daughter is a walking bungalow, full to the brim with *baby* and as tired as another rerun of *Escape to the Country*. So, I'm **on standby**, primed, and ready to rush over to look after my granddaughter, once labour for my girl's second child begins. I can't go to her until she calls, *she says*, because it might not happen until next week after all, *she says*.

(NEXT WEEK! - She 'll self-combust before NEXT WEEK, FFS!). She wants to spend this last bit of time one-to-one with her first daughter whilst the little one is still an '*only*', *she says*, before she must divide attention between two. So, I'm **on standby**. But she surely can't hold on much longer, she's a water-retaining hormonal tsunami, a puffy Piñata stuffed ready to explode. Birthing is problematic for the women in our family. And I'm sinking here- every nerve and sinew strung as taut as the washing line I hoisted at 5.30 am this morning - and exhausted just holding all the snaky worries that coil and snarl in a basket in my head. And the phone is ringing...

and I savage the cold-calling insulation salesman, mercilessly slicing and dicing him down the line, before ending the call abruptly. Find myself crying into the third cup of tea of the morning, that I'm cradling, still **on standby**.   And the phone is ringing...

ALL PRAISE TO TAWERET

(Inspired by a sculpture of an Egyptian Hippopotamus, circa 1880 BC, a symbolic figure honouring the Egyptian goddess of childbirth and fertility. (Held in the Sainsbury Centre, Norwich)

They say you are *ground quartz faience,* and though aged to softer hue,
at origin you were lustrous green and all tjehenet*, *dazzling brightness,*
adorned with marsh waterlilies which, closing at dusk
and re-opening every morning, symbolised regeneration, rebirth -
All praise to Taweret, Great One, Lady of Heaven, Mistress of Pure Water.

Smooth curves, stocky legs striding purposefully forward, powerful head -
you appear deceptively benign, but gaze and stance look to heart of the matter-
hold quiet strength, a hint of silent challenge - as deep within, ancient magic
still curls, is still potent, imbued as you are to evoke Taweret's powers -
All praise to Taweret, Great One, Lady of Heaven, Mistress of Pure Water.

When your kind swam the Nile, feared as life-takers, destroyers
of crops, watercraft- even thought to threaten those last journeys,
to afterlife - you demanded appeasement.
Yet your apotropaic aspect, as symbol of goddess,
all praise to Taweret, Great One, Lady of Heaven, Mistress of Pure Water-
bringer of fertility, guardian of birthing, and child rearing-
that demanded more – demanded reverence - as protector.
All praise to Taweret, Great One, Lady of Heaven, Mistress of Pure Water.

And here, in your present tranquil solitude, I wonder
how many you have safely guided into being? And if, perhaps,
a little magic can be spared for my child, who comes to term soon?
For the women in our family   do not birth easily.
All praise to Taweret, Great One, Lady of Heaven, Mistress of Pure Water.

Notes: * tjehenet, - 'dazzling', 'brilliant', to describe the material we now call Egyptian faience
* Taweret (or Taurt, Tuat, Tuart, Ta-weret, Tawaret, Twert, Taueret- protective Ancient Egyptian goddess of childbirth and fertility. *apotropaic-'causing things to turn away' or 'intended to ward off evil'

MATERNAL CONNECTIONS

The umbilical cord might be cut
but is never truly sundered-
just rendered invisible,
but is tightened on need
and pullable from either end,
like a Christmas cracker.

And that essential link extends
through my children
to theirs -
a mind-walloping, gut-wrenching tether
that bowls me over with that
I know you and I would know you anywhere-
would die before letting anyone ever hurt you
recognition,
that holding of them in my heart-safe.

So, when my son or daughter says
I never understood just how much
I would love this little babe –
how wondrous-amazing he/she is,
I say - *perhaps now*
you can begin to see
just how I feel about you -
and these babes of yours-
and find it impossible to understand
why my own mother
rarely seemed to feel this way.

DEFAULT SETTING

A shrill scream slices through the cold air-
and adult heads all swiftly lift and turn
as one, eyes cut to the swings,
capture the moment of spill as the toddler tumbles,
a crumpled, bottom upmost, ball of wail.
We see spreading red stains on grit-studded hands, grimy, be-holed tights -
the mother kneels in grey slush, uprights her child,
holds, rocks, comforts, calms, kisses better.

Instantly all the women in or near the play park –
the mothers
of toddlers, teens, or, like me, a parent of parents -
stand rigid, a hand pressing each stomach-
gulping in air, as if punched in the gut,
body thrumming with remembered adrenalin rush,
of panicked moments stretched to palpitating lifetimes
when their babies lay similarly sprawled.

After that frozen forever/fleeting pause we smile stiffly, nod,
sever that brief linking that bound us all, with inane comments,
like *gravity's a bugger, eh*? - but raw with recognition
that, regardless of age, or all the other faces we may wear - *Mum*
is incised deep internally as an automatic default,
written through us as indelibly as in holiday resort sticks of rock.
And for some of us older ones - we stride off in a chill blast of nostalgia -
for days when we could always make it better with a kiss.

POLICE UNIFORMS

1. 5 am and the doorbell electrifies me **awake**,
   jerks me fumble-footed downstairs.
   Bleary-eyed, I open the door - to
   wall-to-wall police uniforms,
   a human jigsaw puzzle of black and white,
   from turtle-like body armour to pinched, pale, faces
   creased with exhaustion, propped on the doorframe, backlit
   by the flashing blue light on the drive behind them.

   Only with a croaked *Mum?* from a puffed, misshapen head,
   hanging down mid-block, did I recognise my own son, realised
   he was held horizontally by three other officers.
   Gathering wits with my dressing gown and tying all together,
   I stepped back. They carried him in, tenderly, carefully as a cracked egg,
   muttering quietly as they laid him down, *Sorry 'bout this Mrs F.*
   Had to bring him - no beds, no ambulances. Couldn't leave him there -
   before sideling out, shaking off thanks like drops from a dog's coat.

2. My boy fell asleep with his head in my lap
   as I picked pieces of gravel from boot-shaped indentations.
   He'd been jumped on, kicked, stamped on, by six drunks
   on Norwich's *Street of Dreams* - whilst trying to save their first victim's life
   knowing to wait for back up would risk the man's life.

3. Two operations-and three years on,
   he puts on badge and uniform every day, does his job,
   but he'll never be fully fit again. No-one paid any price for that night
   but him - and the taxpayers, covering his wage as he mended, over six months.
   The victim he saved, *Never ask'd no fucking copper to help him, after all!*
   After a court hearing, one of the thugs approached my son,
   having suddenly realised he had been at school with him-
   Nothin' personal mate - didn't see it was you- just saw another Pig.

4. Some see the police as sadistic, bully boys, abusing their power,
   because the media only highlights the bad apples amongst them.
   Look behind the uniform. Each one is worn by someone's child,
   or partner, or parent. It's not there to make them faceless
   or intimidating, but so you can find one when you need help –
           (and if you need a police officer it's always in a hurry),
   It's there to soak up the inevitable stench and spills of crime,
           (I know, I've washed them out on occasion).
   But uniforms can be seen as a target – and when a one is put on,
   somewhere a mother holds their breath, in equal parts of pride and fear,
   and sometimes poems are written to hold a mother's burning wrath.

THE BITTER TRUTH OF MOTHERING AN ADULT CHILD IN PAIN

Bleak-faced, he stands silent, head bowed, shoulders hunched,
like weathered, ancient stone - bunched and eroded by the onslaught
of pernicious lashing tides.
I try to comfort him
as serpentine creatures' writhe through my mind
sorting and sifting potential causes for his grief-heave,
offer unconditional love; my arms encircle him-
soft but steady, soothing, calm- exuding tenderness,
feather finger-stoke his back, slowly touch-kiss his hair,
while he lets me -
just being there, listening, holding -
not asking, not prying

until the silently imploding kerosene keg of hurt
eventually subsides
enough for him to step back, breathe deep, pull together,
quietly murmur, *But I thought she loved me, Mum,*
and my heart also breaks, for him.

I am a constant, to help him regain and maintain balance
when he can accept support, and at his own pace-
the raw and bitter truth of mothering an adult child in pain -
but take pride from his quiet dignity,
and know, like stone - he will endure,
will slowly regather strength to eventually embrace new loves -
wholeheartedly.

SHE STANDS STRONG

inspired by Venus of Willendorf, artist unknown, 30,000 BC

A pocket-sized essence of motherhood,
endurance written along every voluptuous fold.
A simple no nonsense carving - but as straightforward
and eye-stopping as your gaze,
though that warm, sensuous texture
deliberately made a mere handful
calls fingers to fondle, to clasp.

How your maker must have held you
in reverence, in necessity,
to have created you so petite, so portable,
so pleasingly rounded, to fit so perfectly
that a hand in a pocket could caress you,
take quiet anonymous comfort in your constancy–
there when needed.

You evidence your nurturing, solace giving nature –
gravity-pulled pendulous breasts and distended stomach,
badges of honour, on legs that struggle to support you,
yet you stand erect, ooze quiet strength,
confidence, ready to take on what comes.
Still beautiful in the eyes of your beholders
no matter how many years pass-

a minute embodiment of every mother
that has stood proud, made clear-
I know my role and worth- this is me- let me help you.

SALT

The knives are always out for Lot's wife,
archaic acrimony ripping through her reputation like a dose of salts
jumping to assumptions, about why she chose to disobey angelic demands -
looked back.

Lot's wife- not even dignified with her own name,
harried from her home, briny tears stinging her face,
body slick and stinking with sweat - no time
to gather thoughts, treasures salted away over the years,
nod a farewell to familiar surroundings, or, most poignantly,
ensure her daughters followed close
before her god declared open season on Sodom –
she **had** to look back,
what woman, what mother, worth her salt, wouldn't?

We mothers *season* others daily, invest in making life more palatable
nurture health, heal with light kisses, try to preserve peace
in a world awash with a brackish sea of dissipating foamy values
and sprays of saline-crusted question marks all nibbling at the future.
Perhaps because, instinctively,
we look back,
try to learn from mistakes?

We come from salt, end as salt-
that tangible symbol of friendship, spiritual energy,
seal of agreements for centuries - so surely, becoming a pillar of salt
is more salute than punishment?

I stand with Lot's wife, aspirational salt of the earth
                Don't call me *Honey*
                Don't call me *Sugar*
                If you must, just call me *Salt*.

A WINDOW FOR BREAKFAST

takes time and patience -
        gather it up carefully from the edges
        pull it together with some intricate folding
        *(the corners **are** a bit tricky to be honest)*-
        until the whole thing can be crammed intact
        into my mouth, and swallow
        down with a mug of strong breakfast tea

As it springs back into shape
I feel the burgeoning of those carefully selected items
I placed in the frame yesterday –
        family, lawn-sprawled, laughing
        at the babies splashing in the paddling pool,
        gasping at the shock-shiver sheer wetness of water
                one cat tail-flicking in irritation at nap disturbance
                the other fleeing from arcs of splash,
                last of the picnic debris awash on the blanket
        three generations making time for each other
                amid kite flying
                the admiring of bird clouds
                and extracting the littles from the new flower beds

and I rub my stomach gently, feeling a slight indigestion
        (probably the kite strings getting twisted)
but happily, full -
        knowing I can now keep it forever
        to lick on chill lonely days.

GET BENEATH HER SKIN

after And the Soul - Kim Moore

if you really want to know her,
meet her with open palms
as she moon-bathes in lull of night
and as she opens, unfurls like a waterlily to restore, take blessing-
gaze at the creature coiled inside –

if a shy, bemused mouse
let her run back to nest, pretend you have not seen her
in kindness, so she can continue in quiet busyness

if a self-absorbed, sun-worshiper of a cat
fuss her, feed her – but don't believe a word
she says, she will flirt with anyone

if a chocolate-eyed, long lash-ed cow sit for a comfortable catch up
but do not stay too long – her gossip will be all pasture and cud
and will turn your brain to hay mush

but take great care if this mamma harbours a slumbering tiger
in the jungle of her heart, who will scent lies and disloyalty
as easy prey and with provocation will rise
claws unsheathed, sabre-sharp teeth bared,
ready to slash and maim
any that threaten her or hers -

for when roused, without doubt, Tiger Mammas
are the most dangerous creatures on the planet.
But if you are strong enough, brave enough, rise too –
join with us other tigers in shared voice as we crouch in watchfulness,
deep inside - for we lay in wait in the most unexpected lairs,
and rend the fulsome dark with warning song.

ULTIMATELY A MOTHER IS A PAPERCLIP -

if you have children
you keep going, you endure
do whatever it takes

you hold them clasped
always, give context, lend strength,
separate, yet bound

but let your babies fly
as nest confines, wings flutter,
ease from your grasp

always you hold all
that epitomises love,
home, safety, warmth, care

pinned in your heart-safe -
keep love, and home, handy- for
whenever needed